Dear Chris,
    Happy Chri
I hope you enjo...........
    but still have time for me!
    lots and lots of love,
        Charly xxx

BATH TRAMWAYS

Series editor Robert J Harley

Peter Davey
Paul Welland

MP Middleton Press

To Teresa, Su and Tony Davey

To Barbara, Zoe and Jamie Welland

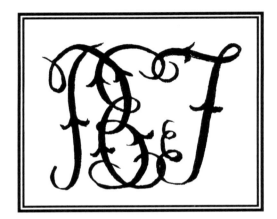

Published October 1996

ISBN 1 873793 84 7

© Middleton Press 1996

Design - Deborah Goodridge

Published by Middleton Press
Easebourne Lane
Midhurst
West Sussex
GU29 9AZ
Tel: 01730 813169
Fax: 01730 812601

Printed & bound by Biddles Ltd,
Guildford and Kings Lynn

CONTENTS

TRAM ROUTES

1 - Bathford - Guildhall - Combe Down
2 - GWR Station - Kingsmead Square - Upper Bristol Road - Newton St.Loe
3 - GWR Station - Kingsmead Square - Upper Bristol Road - Weston
4 - Guildhall - Lower Bristol Road - Twerton
5 - Guildhall - Old Bridge - Oldfield Park (Cynthia Road)

INTRODUCTION AND ACKNOWLEDGEMENTS

Having sorted through photographs taken by my father, S.Miles Davey, for the Bristol book in this series, I came across some negatives of the Bath system. But, whilst thinking I had not enough material for a Bath volume, I remembered Paul Welland had collected a wonderful selection of views. He kindly agreed to assist and so this joint publication has been born.

I would like to thank *The Bath Chronicle*, Bath Reference Library for supplying copies of the maps they hold, Messrs. Gerald Bath, C.Carter, Colin Maggs and H.B.Priestley for the use of their photographs to complete the story; John Gillham for his superb map of the system in the late 1930s; Paul Welland for his line drawings; and the late John Appleby, W.A.Camwell, my father Miles Davey, W.S.Eades, S.G.Jackman, M.J.O'Connor, G.N.Southerden and Bill Vaughan-Jenkins for having the foresight to record such splendid moments photographically and yet unable to witness their work in this volume.

My sincere thanks to Donald Packham for his invaluable assistance in preparing and typing the text. Lastly to my wife, Teresa, who was bombed out whilst living in the Royal Crescent, for checking dates and various historical facts.

PETER DAVEY

I would like to take this opportunity to thank my friend Peter Davey of Bristol for including me in this volume of *Tramway Classics*, and for his help with my hobby and for making a dream come true.

My thanks also to work colleague Brian K.Lewis of Peasedown for his photographic expertise, Mrs E.Derrick, G.Drew, A.Gallop and Wilf Gingell.

We are grateful to G.Croughton for providing most of the tickets.

Lastly to my wife, Barbara, for her patience and understanding whilst I have been collecting for so many years.

PAUL WELLAND

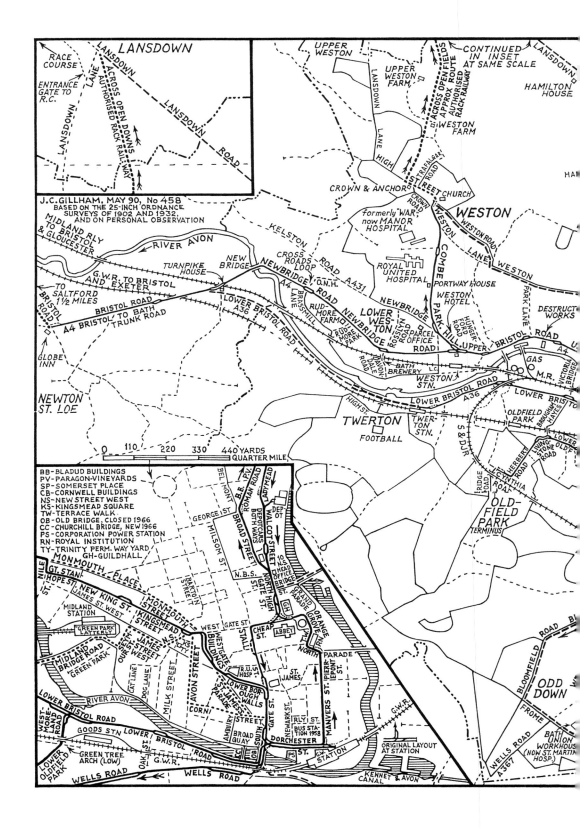

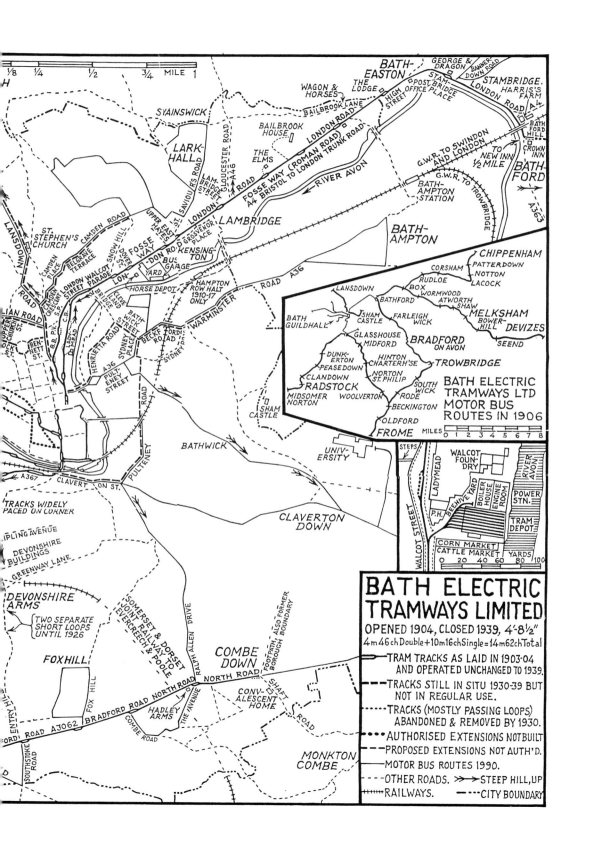

BATH ELECTRIC TRAMWAYS LTD MOTOR BUS ROUTES IN 1906

BATH ELECTRIC TRAMWAYS LIMITED

OPENED 1904, CLOSED 1939, 4'-8½"
4m 46ch Double + 10m 16ch Single = 14m 62ch Total

— TRAM TRACKS AS LAID IN 1903-04
AND OPERATED UNCHANGED TO 1939.

─ ─ TRACKS STILL IN SITU 1930-39 BUT
NOT IN REGULAR USE.

······ TRACKS (MOSTLY PASSING LOOPS)
ABANDONED & REMOVED BY 1930.

•—•—• AUTHORISED EXTENSIONS NOT BUILT

─ ─ PROPOSED EXTENSIONS NOT AUTH'D.

── MOTOR BUS ROUTES 1990.

─·─·─ OTHER ROADS. ≫≫ STEEP HILL, UP

++++++ RAILWAYS. ─··─ CITY BOUNDARY

GEOGRAPHICAL SETTING

The City of Bath was situated in the County of Somerset with the City of Bristol to the west and a rather hilly town of Bradford on Avon to the east. The River Avon runs through the centre of the city under the famous Pulteney Bridge, designed by Robert Adam and built between 1769 and 1774. Even today, it is still beautifully lined on both sides with shops but it was his only work in Bath.

The Ordnance Survey maps used are to the scale of 25 inches to the mile (1: 2500) and are dated 1932 unless otherwise stated.

HISTORICAL BACKGROUND

Bath Abbey is situated on the same site as that of an early Saxon Cathedral and Monastery. It was here that Edgar was crowned the first King of All England in 973 AD, later it also became the site for a Norman Cathedral. Elizabeth I visited Bath in 1574 and she was so shocked at the condition of the building, that she immediately ordered "national funding to pay for repairs to such a beautiful abbey." The city also houses the famous Roman Baths built about 1100, which King Bladud of Athens is reported to have discovered. Other local landmarks are the terrace and surrounding colonnade, to the design of J.M.Brydon, the beautiful Georgian Royal Crescent, designed by John Wood the younger and built between 1767 and 1775, his famous Queen Square and lastly his unique Circus.

The first horse tram service began in 1880 and consisted of only one route, which started from the GWR Station. It ran via Southgate Street, High Street and Walcot to Grosvenor. The horse stables and depot were situated at the rear of the Porter Butt Hotel, London Road.

On 2nd January 1904, electric traction began using the standard gauge of four feet eight and a half inches/1435mm. To get the tramway up and running, R.D.McCarter, an American, was appointed as the Company's first General Manager and Engineer. His duties were taken over in 1908 by W.E.Hardy. There were 40 cars in total of Milnes' construction: 1-34 double deck and 50-55 single deck. The latter were often known as whippets. Cars 1-18 and 50-51 were used for the opening, and the remaining trams were delivered in August of the same year. The reason for the six single deck cars being ordered was to enable trams to run under the low railway bridge in Westmoreland Road on the route to Oldfield Park.

Unusually for a city layout, there were two different one-way systems. One was relatively simple, being out via Broad Street and in via Walcot Street. The other amazingly ran around the city centre in an anti-clockwise manner from Dorchester Street, GWR Station, Guildhall/Abbey and back through Cheap Street, Stall Street and Southgate Street.

The service ceased on Saturday, 6th May 1939 with Car 22 doing the honours. Driven by the Mayor, Captain Adrian Hopkins, and assisted by Chief Inspector Hale at the helm, she left promptly from the Guildhall at midnight with one hundred passengers on board. Special tickets were issued and put in souvenir wallets. Sadly, she made history by becoming the last passenger car to operate, fighting the crowds on the way back to the only depot, in Walcot Street. Nearly all the trams were broken up at the Glasshouse sidings opposite St. Martin's Hospital, Midford Road, with the remainder being scrapped at the depot.

Luckily the depot survives today, used as a market on Saturdays and a car park during the week. Apart from this building, little remains to remind us of a once well maintained fleet and an efficient service that crossed the city so faithfully for 35 years.

BATHFORD - GUILDHALL

1. We start our first journey from the eastern side of Bath, where Car 8 waits at the Bathford terminus outside the Crown public house on the 18th April 1938. Note the trolley pole reverser on the overhead and also the dangerous arrangement whereby passengers board in the middle of the road. Note also the errant motorist who is undertaking a risky overtaking manoeuvre on the wrong side of the road. (W.A.Camwell)

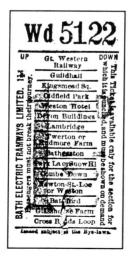

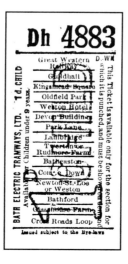

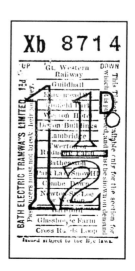

2. A little way along from the previous view, Car 28 is loading at the transfer station for the omnibus (FB 05, Milnes Daimler) to Chippenham. The tram will then proceed beneath the GWR bridge to terminate outside the Crown Inn. The Pepper Pot tower can be seen on the sky line; the date is circa 1910.
(Bath Reference Library)

<table>
<tr><td colspan="3">Ce 9900</td></tr>
</table>

	1d	
Bathford		Devonshire Blgs.
Bath easton		Plough Inn
Clarence Gardens	Bath Electric Tramways Ltd. This Ticket is available ONLY for section indicated by punch, must be retained INTACT and shewn on demand. Issued subject to Bye-laws.	Glass-house
Lam-bridge		Combe Road
Cleve-land Bridge		Combe Down
Guild-hall		Snow Hill
Old Bridge		Top Broad Street
Upp. Oldfield Park		Single
Hunt, Hucknall Rd, Nottm.		

<table>
<tr><td colspan="3">Wd 1185</td></tr>
</table>

	1d	
G.W.R. Station		Guild-hall
Nile Street		Brougham Hayes
Weston Hotel	Bath Electric Tramways Ltd. This Ticket is available ONLY for section indicated by punch. Must be retained INTACT and shewn on demand. Issued subject to Bye-laws.	Green Tree
X Roads Loop		Twerton
Weston Term.		Stanley Road
Turn-pike		Oldfield Park
Newton St. Loe		Single
Hunt, H.		ll Rd, Nottm.

3. London Road is depicted at the turn of the century with Batheaston Congregational Church standing in the background. This location is known as Stambridge and shows the passing loop outside the White Lion Inn. The tram is heading for Bathford having come from the city. (P.G.Davey Coll.)

4. Car 17, destined for Combe Down, eases her way past the Lamb & Flag public house, while going through the High Street in Batheaston. The locals seem amused to see the situation being recorded. (P.C.Welland Coll.)

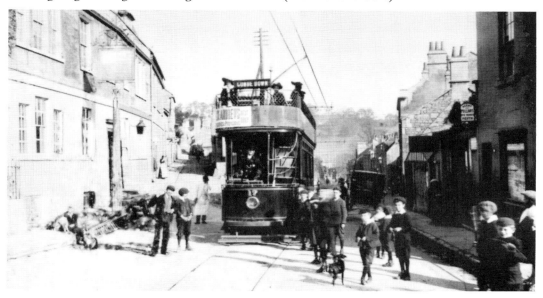

5. Having climbed up from Bailbrook College, Car 31 awaits at the transfer station stop, opposite the then Rich & Cooling Nurseries. Note the row of overhead traction poles used on this stretch of road.
(C.G.Maggs Coll.)

6. Car 8, on a short working to Glasshouse, stands outside the grounds of Bailbrook College. It is thought that this was taken whilst the Bath Horse Show was taking place as special cars were supplied for the extra crowds. The conductor is eyeing up the photographer.
(M.J.O'Connor)

7. Car 34, the highest numbered double deck, is seen at Lambridge terminus outside the Bath Horse Show grounds. Note the Bath Fire Brigade Ambulance in attendance and the Charlie Chaplin look alike policeman busy on point duty at the Gloucester Road junction. This show was held every September for many years. (W.Vaughan-Jenkins)

8. In about 1908, looking in the other direction towards Grosvenor, Car 2 is seen on a short working to Devonshire Arms. In later years of tramway operation this was changed to read DEVONSHIRE BDGS (Buildings). The raised pavement behind the tram is unaltered to this day. (C.Carter Coll.)

9. Track laying is photographed at Grosvenor during the spring of 1903, looking towards Lambridge. Interestingly there seems to be no mechanical means of assistance in the construction, but nevertheless, the finished work was faultless. (P.C.Welland Coll.)

10. Car 13, Bathford bound, passes Kensington Nurseries on London Road. On the horizon can be seen Camden Crescent. Today, Kensington bus depot is a little way down on the left. (P.C.Welland Coll.)

Bath Electric Tramways Ltd.
This ticket was issued on the last tramcar operated at Bath on Saturday, 6th. May 1939.
The car was driven by
Captain Adrian Hopkins M.C., J.P.
Mayor of Bath.

11. In London Street, another view of track laying shows how labour intensive this task was. During this work the Cleveland Toll Bridge was temporarily freed of tolls. In contrast to the new construction in the foreground, older properties are being demolished behind the advertisement hoarding.
(C.G.Maggs Coll.)

→

12. At the same location as above, an unidentified car slopes down towards Walcot Street. Note the lattice gate beside the driver to stop unauthorised entry by passengers, and also the greatcoats hanging under the staircase. The Company supplied these garments to the crews. (G.N.Southerden)

→

13. Car 24 is passing Hedgemead Park and is just about to drop down into London Street on her short working to Lambridge. On this car there appears to be no pattern painted on the stair risers (compare with picture 7).
(P.C.Welland Coll.)

14. We arrive at the depot in Walcot Street at 4.05pm one afternoon in 1939. The depot facade acts as a backdrop to cars 4,32,16,14,1,50 and 22 just after the closure of the system. This picture also shows the lovely array of trackwork. (S.Miles Davey)

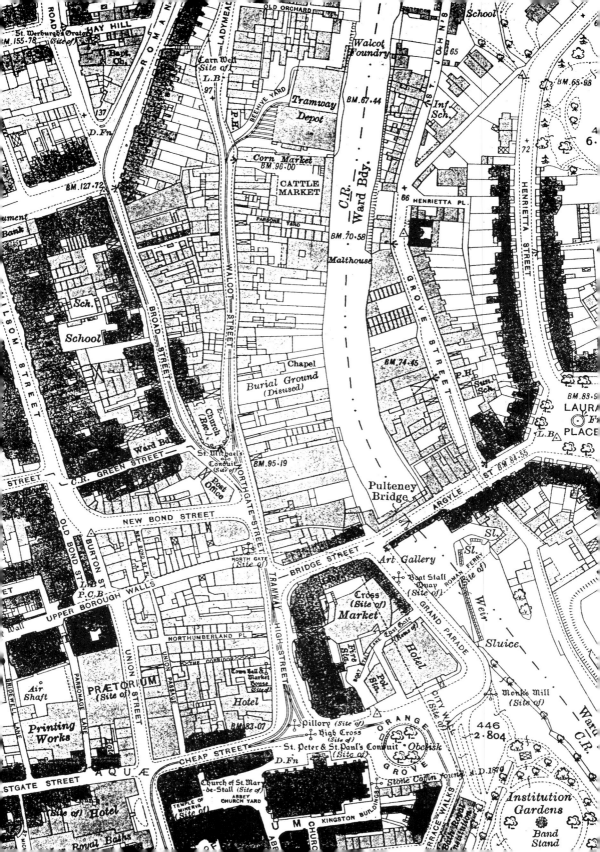

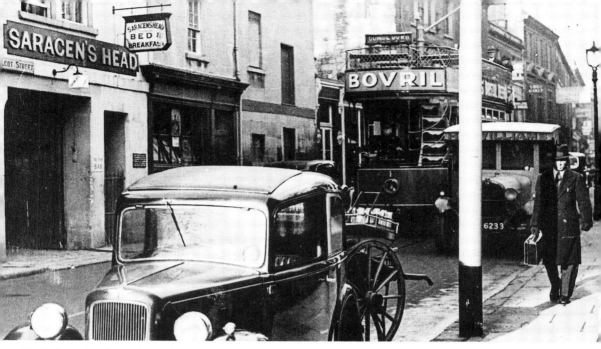

15. Below the depot in Walcot Street car 1 is seen about to pass the Saracen's Head public house en route to Combe Down. Note a milkman's handcart behind the Austin 7. The build-ings behind the tram have now disappeared due to the recent arrival of Saracen Street. (Bath Reference Library)

16. With St. Michael's Church centre stage car 20 enters Northgate Street on a short working to Devonshire Arms. On the left can be seen the track for the outgoing cars which had to use Broad Street. Note the original higher position of the destination boxes which were lowered in 1909. (P.C.Welland Coll.)

17. This lovely view of Broad Street shows possibly car 3 nearing the summit on this one way system for tramcars. In front of the car in the distance can be seen Lansdown Road which by 1908 was worked by buses, leaving the Guildhall ten times a day. The rosettes on the buildings, to hold the overhead, were partly paid for by the shopowners rather than have the traction poles outside their premises. (Bath Reference Library)

18. A view of Northgate Street shows single deck car 53 coming from the depot and destined for Oldfield Park. Double deck Car 20 on a short working to Glasshouse is glimpsed behind. On closer examination we see the motorman about to alight from the single deck. This was not the terminal stop, so we can only assume he will be going into the Company's offices which were at No.10, that is immediately to the right of Horton Brothers, House Furnishers. To the left was Rich & Coolings, who sold seeds, plants and trees. These have all been swept away for the present day Podium Shopping Centre which houses the City Central Library. St. Michael's Church stands to the left and in the foreground is the entrance to the General Post Office which is sited on the corner of New Bond Street. Note another single deck, car 51, no doubt also approaching from Walcot Street Depot.
(BANESC Archive Dept.)

19. Having arrived at the central stop in the High Street outside the Guildhall, car 7 prepares to depart for Combe Down. On the left is the Company's horsedrawn tower wagon in use for maintaining the overhead. (P.G.Davey Coll.)

20. The conductor of car 19 still finds time to give directions to a passenger, as he copes with the chore of turning the trolley pole for the return journey. (C.Carter Coll.)

21. Viewed from the opposite direction, the famous Bath Abbey makes a classic back drop for car 17 bound for Lambridge and another one going to Combe Down. This picture seems to sum up Bath's history in 1935. (Bath Reference Library)

COMBE DOWN - GUILDHALL

22. Starting at the most southerly point on the system, we see car 27 at the terminus in 1937 with the destination linen yet to be changed. The lady is thought to be the photographer's wife with their son. (M.J.O'Connor)

23. At the same location, but viewed from the other direction, is car 33 waiting at Rainbow Woods to cross the city back to Bathford, on 18th April 1938. What a tranquil setting this picture makes, only a few minutes from the city. (W.A.Camwell)

24. At Glasshouse terminus, Midford Road, stands car 30. Whilst the conductor is turning the trolley pole, passengers are helping each other board. Behind the house in the far distance, two sidings were laid in 1939, being the location where the majority of the tramcars were broken up. To the left of the picture out of view is St. Martin's Hospital.
(W. Vaughan-Jenkins)

25. Cars 21 and 2 halt at the top of Wellsway, both trams are on their way to Combe Down around 1904. It is thought that this was a posed view taken for publicity reasons, because this location was not a terminus. The two inspectors are Messrs Hale and McConnochie who are with Motorman Callan and Conductor Poole.
(Bristol Tramways & Carriage Co. Ltd.)

26. Coming down the hill we reach Bear Flat before the line was doubled. Bloomfield Road goes off to the right and at the top of Wellsway a tram stands outside Devonshire Buildings in the distance. (P.G.Davey Coll.)

27. Car 2 waits on Bear Flat whilst on a short working to Lambridge. The JCR 24 Hour News & Food shop now occupies the site where Alexandra Dairies once stood. (C.G.Maggs Coll.)

28. Looking back on Bear Flat from the top of Wells Road, we see car 8 about to take the sharp left turn on her way down to the city. The motorman has his white topped summer cover placed on his company issue cap. (P.C.Welland Coll.)

29. Many interesting forms of transport in 1935 make a lovely picture with car 27 passing the Royal Sailor public house, on her short working to Devonshire Buildings. She has just passed under the GWR bridge which took trains to London and Bristol. The tram tracks on the right are used by single deck cars to Oldfield Park and double deckers to Twerton. (Bath Reference Library)

30. Having dropped down about 500 feet/152 metres from the terminus at Combe Down, we reach the city by crossing the River Avon over the Old Bridge. The cars will then turn right into Dorchester Street and head towards the GWR Station. In the distance is the famous Abbey and St.James' Church.
(P.C.Welland Coll.)

31. Car 25 is caught on camera at Terrace Walk and is Bathford bound. The date is 8th October 1937, which means that this vehicle has only nineteen months' service left. She passes Bath Tramways' AEC motor bus, GL5084. The destination signs on these buses were known as *Bible Boards*. Bath Abbey can be seen behind the other buildings.
(J.B.Appleby Coll.)

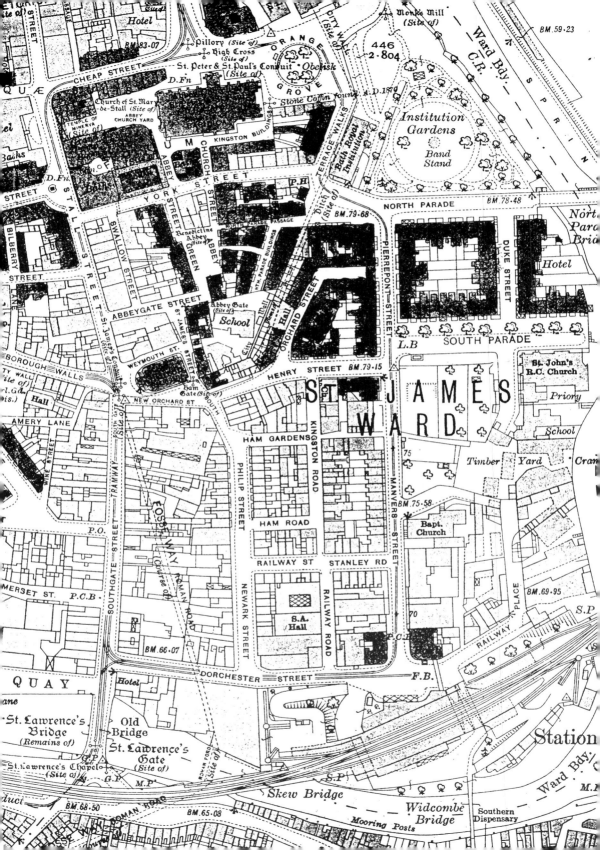

32. Having negotiated Terrace Walk car 27 enters Orange Grove and will proceed in a "Keep Right" direction, even though banned for other vehicular traffic. Although the picture was taken pre-war, the scene has hardly changed to this day. (W.S.Eades)

TO School	FROM School
Monday	
Tuesday	
Wednesday	
Thursday	
Friday	
Saturday	

BATH ELECTRIC TRAMWAYS, LTD.

SCHOLAR'S WEEKLY TRAVEL TKT.

7½d.

Available over a 1rd. section as shown on Scholar's Demand Ticket. No allowance for Lost Journeys. Issued subject to the Company's Bye-laws and Conditions.

C 15501

BATH TRAMWAYS MOTOR CO., LTD.

Scholar's Weekly Travel Tickets

FARE

Available over section as shown on Scholar's Demand Card. No allowance for lost journeys. Issued subject to the Rules and Bye-laws of the Company.

8501

33. The Abbey appears again behind the city's central stop where car 25 has pulled up outside the Guildhall. (P.C.Welland Coll.)

34. Awaiting in front of the City's historic Abbey, in 1935, are examples of the only two types of car used on this system. Cars 1 and 54 are at the terminus. The single deck is about to turn right into Cheap Street whilst the double deck seems to be encouraging passengers to board quickly for a short working to Glasshouse, leaving the police constable to do the military two step. (P.G.Davey Coll.)

35. At the same location, passengers have alighted from car 25 which is about to return to Glasshouse on 10th September 1937. (H.B.Priestley)

36. Viewed the other way, car 26 waits to depart by going via Cheap Street on the one way system that tramcars had to traverse when going south. The motorman is wearing mittens. (W.Vaughan-Jenkins)

37. Entering Cheap Street is car 19 on a short working to Glasshouse; on the right is a Bristol K5G double decker (DKN 46, ex Chatham & District) on route 5. Buses replaced the trams to Twerton on 22nd April 1939. (D.Withers Coll.)

38. Stall Street was unusually a one way thoroughfare for trams during normal operational hours, but it was used in both directions before 7.45 in the morning, so as not to disturb residents in hotels in Manvers and Pierrepont Streets. When the trams went round into Cheap Street, it was imperative that the conductor walked in front to ensure no tram was coming the other way. Our picture shows a tram coming up into the passing loop which might well be early on a summer morning. On the right is Bath Street and also the Mineral Water Fountain can just be seen. This was later dismantled and is now to be found at Terrace Walk. (P.G.Davey Coll.)

39. Coming to the end of the one way system, the junction for Lower Borough Walls can be seen for the Newton and Weston routes. Car 26 approaches towards the camera. (P.C.Welland Coll.)

NEWTON - GWR STATION

40. Trees make a very peaceful setting for car 12 at Newton terminus. Her crew includes Motorman C.Lye and Conductor C.Tozer who pose for the photographer. The year is 1935 and the Globe Inn still survives today, but with a large roundabout outside. (S.G.Jackman)

41. This time we are at the same spot, but looking back towards the city. The rural nature of this scene is enhanced by the herd of cattle and the hedge lined meadows in the valley of the Avon. Spring sunshine catches car 25 as she is made ready for the return to the GWR Station. Note the number of traction poles needed for this stretch of track. (P.C.Welland Coll.)

42. The stone wall seems to have gone into decline as we view the same location on 18th April 1938. The conductor is just coming down the staircase. It is almost impossible to imagine that this is the main A4 road to Bristol which is now a dual carriageway with an abundance of heavy traffic. Note the automatic trolley reverser to the right of the car. (W.A.Camwell)

43. Car 22 crests the Newbridge in 1935. The weekday service west of New Bridge Cross Roads loop was a car every thirty minutes, hence there was no need for signals as only one tram was timetabled to be on this single track section at any particular time. (S.G.Jackman)

44. On her return journey we observe a tram which will eventually terminate at the GWR Station. She crosses the Newbridge on 19th January 1938; the River Avon flows sedately past. (G.Mortimer)

45. Further along from the previous view in Newbridge Road we see car 20 ambling towards the city. Nowadays this has become rather a built up area with Rudmore Park to the left. Most of the houses to the right are now hotels and B&B establishments.
(P.C.Welland Coll.)

46. We are now at the Lower Weston side of Newbridge Road, this time with car 18. There has been little change to this location with the Post Office and Station Road to the left and Chelsea Road to the right. Note the baker's boy poised with his basket. He is not far from his employment as the Old Red House Bakery was situated to the left behind the camera. (P.G.Davey Coll.)

47. At the junction outside the Weston Hotel the routes from Newton and Weston now join and car 24 approaches from Newbridge Hill. Many of the earlier advertisements were split in two at the ends but this was discontinued in the later years of operation. (P.G.Davey Coll.)

48. The backdrop to this scene is the Cliff View Hotel and Restaurant which was situated at the junction of Dorchester Street and Southgate Street. The unidentified double deck tram turns into Dorchester Street nearing the end of her journey which will be outside the GWR Station. At the same time car 28 comes towards the camera out of Southgate Street on a short working to Glasshouse, and will soon cross the Old Bridge. On the horizon can be seen St.James' Church. (G.N.Southerden)

49. Coming through Dorchester Street, a Newton bound car is about to pass an interesting assortment of vehicles which includes a Stanley Marks bread van. This picture gives a clear view of the rails at the junction and the electrical feeder wires which supply 550 volts DC to the overhead.
(Bath Reference Library)

50. From a different vantage point we see part of the facade of the GWR Station. Car 12's linen blind is changed ready for her return journey to Newton. She carries an advertisement for Bath Garages - ironically the internal combustion engine was the very invention that caused the demise for most British tramway systems. Also advertised is that famous Bristol Brewery; this would have been a red background with white lettering. (Dr. Richards)

OLDFIELD PARK - GUILDHALL

51. Here we see car 54 at the terminus in Cynthia Road by Mayfield Road. The date is 18th April 1938 and the destination blind has yet to be changed to GUILDHALL for the return journey. The points bar can be seen leaning against the interior of the dash by the controller handle. The shop on the corner of Mayfield Road has since become a private residence now occupied by co-author, Paul Welland's brother-in-law. (W.A.Camwell)

52. From the reverse view we see the highest numbered of the single deckers, car 55, at the terminus. This photo was taken in the 1920s before the bulkhead end windows were fitted. This work was carried out around 1929 and that section of the car was used by smokers. Note the early route plate 3 hanging above the driver, these were phased out around 1930. The bamboo pole lying above the truck would be used whenever the trolley had to be moved by hand. (G.N.Southerden)

→

53. From the top of Herbert Road we catch sight of a city bound tram waiting for car 54 to negotiate the crossover. She has just passed Moorland Road and will proceed to the summit of the hill to terminate in Cynthia Road. Her blind has already been changed to read GUILDHALL. (G.N.Southerden)

→

54. A combination car comes into view from Herbert Road on her return to the city. Bystanders seem intrigued by the actions of the photographer who must be standing in the middle of Moorland Road. This picture can be dated in the early 1900s as we can see there are no roof advertisement boards as yet on this car. These were attached later in about February 1909. (P.C.Welland Coll.)

55. Further along from the previous view we are now at Stanley Road West, which is to the left of car 52. She will then proceed across the top of Brougham Hayes and into Lower Oldfield Park on her return to the Guildhall. She advertises Simonds Ales, the colours being dark blue lettering and a red hop leaf on a white background. (W.Vaughan-Jenkins)

56. This is a view of Lower Oldfield Park looking down towards Brougham Hayes. On closer examination we can see an unidentified combination car ambling its way along a tree lined route on its return to the city. (P.G.Davey Coll.)

57. This 1927 view shows car 54 going towards Oldfield Park under the low railway bridge, which was the reason for the purchase of these unusual single decks. Westmoreland Road can be seen at the rear of the car. In two years' time the end bulkhead windows will be fitted. (G.N.Southerden)

58. We are at the Oldfield Park junction where car 55 is about to negotiate the sharp left turn from the Lower Bristol Road into Westmoreland Road. The Green Tree public house is just visible to the right of the picture while the vast factory buildings to the left are the premises of Stothert & Pitt Ltd. The year is 1938. (C.G.Maggs Coll.)

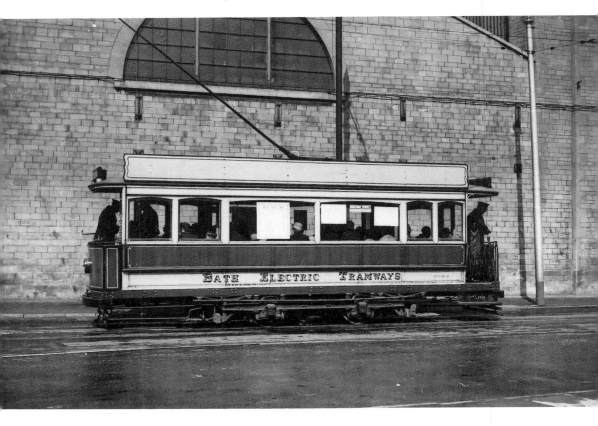

60. A wonderful photograph of Car 50 on 18th April 1938, with Motorman Len Cootes standing proudly at the helm. Many years ago co-author, Paul Welland, had the pleasure of meeting and talking to Len who came to Bath from London in 1926. This view shows the final state of the single deck cars. Duck, Son & Pinker's are still trading today in Bridge Street. (W.A.Camwell)

59. Here on the Lower Bristol Road we have a broadside view of car 50 with the Stothert & Pitt buildings behind. The crew have been forced to wear waterproof clothing after a short, sharp shower. The large advert on the window is for Motor Coach Tours whilst in between the two smaller ones is the sign of things to come, one for National Service. (S.Miles Davey)

61. Further along the Lower Bristol Road, a Bristol A type bus FB 6701 has just reversed in front of car 51 which is on route to Oldfield Park. As we can see by the passengers standing on the platform, she is fully laden after somewhat of an emergency stop for this motorman. Note the company sign on the traction pole which reads CARS STOP HERE IF REQUIRED. The Old Bridge is a little way back to the right of the picture.
(D.Withers Collection)

62. Viewed through the opening of the GWR bridge, we can see car 51 crossing the Old Bridge. At precisely the same position as the preceding motor car, the points will be changed and she will then swing sharp right (left of the picture) along Lower Bristol Road. The track in the foreground will take the Combe Down and short working Glasshouse cars up Wells Road. What a lovely place to put those colourful enamel signs.
(P.G.Davey Coll.)

63. The motorman of car 50 keeps his eye on the traffic coming the other way across the Old Bridge. His car masks another open top vehicle which is heading towards the castellated towers installed by the GWR to make the view of the railway viaduct more aesthetically acceptable. (R.J.Harley Coll.)

64. Car 52 crests the Old Bridge on her way to Oldfield Park. The motorman takes hold of the long points bar and will lean forward over the dash to change them. His waterproof coat hangs by the bulkhead window. The platform lattice gate is closed so that no passenger attempts to board. The original bridge on this site was built on Roman foundations and was known as St.Lawrence's Bridge. By the 19th century it was redesigned and became known as the "Old Bridge" with pierced balustrades and cantilevered footpaths. The structure was demolished in 1966. (C.Carter)

POINTS ALWAYS TO BE REMEMBERED BY MOTORMEN.

(1) In all cases of doubt take the safe course.
(2) Do not run faster than schedule time and pay particular attention to the speed limits allowed by the Board of Trade.

The following table gives speeds in miles per hour, with the corresponding number of poles which are passed while travelling at the respective speeds.

Miles per hour.		Poles passed per minute.
4	..	... 3 approximately.
5	...	... 3¾ ,,
6	...	... 4½ ,,
7	...	... 5¼ ,,
8	...	... 6 ,,
9	...	... 6¾ ,,
10	...	... 7½ ,,
11	...	... 8¼ ,,
12	...	... 9 ,,

(3) Always shut off the current before applying brakes, and always release the brakes before applying the power.
(4) Never run back without reversing the trolley at curves and sections where the trolley pole might get caught in the overhead wires.
Always take the controlling handles with you, while you are in charge, if you leave the platform of the car.
(6) Always bring the car nearly to a stop at the top of all steep gradients, then descend slowly, with the car well under control.
Shut off power, sound gong, and slaken speed as you approach street crossings.
(8 See that the sand hoppers are in order and boxes filled with dry sand.
(9 Never, under any circumstances, run down gradients with the current on, and never stop on a heavy gradient, except when absolutely necessary.

Extract from the handbook issued by BET to all motormen

65. From the end of Southgate Street, double deck Car 16 crosses the Old Bridge for Twerton. After going through the points she will turn sharp right and go the full length of the Lower Bristol Road. The chap crossing the road is Dr Richards who has just managed to avoid being knocked down by Car 55. The single decker is about to turn sharp right into Dorchester Street, which is left of the picture, and make her way toward the Guildhall via Manvers Street. (Dr Richards Coll.)

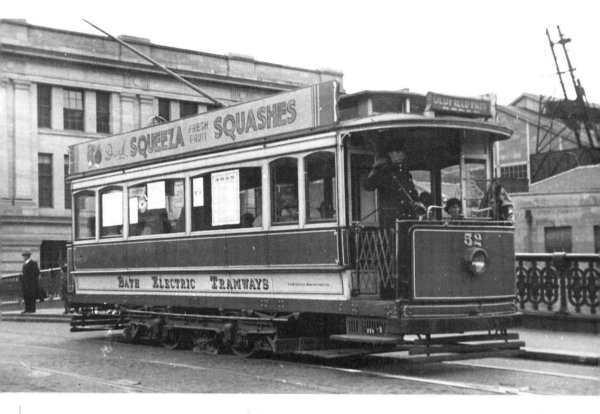

66. We arrive at Orange Grove nearing the journey's end. Car 50 will turn towards the camera followed by the double decker. All routes, except for Newton and Weston, would return on this stretch of track and terminate outside the Guildhall. The newspaper vendor's headlines of 1935 read SWIMMERS DEATH DIVE AT BATHS. (S.G.Jackman)

67. The year is 1935 and car 54 stands in the High Street outside the Guildhall which is to the left of the picture. She will then approach the Abbey and turn right into Cheap Street on her return journey to Oldfield Park. (Dr.Richards)

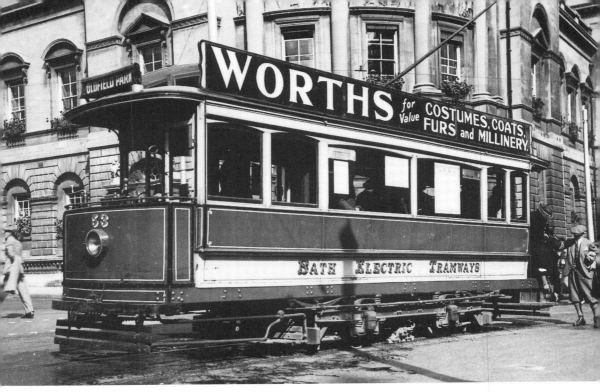

68. Two years on from the previous view on 10th September 1937, we can see from the position of car 53 that the terminal location has been changed to be adjacent to the Abbey. Cheap Street is to the left of the picture and this car will proceed in that direction on route to Oldfield Park. The backdrop is the Guildhall. (H.B.Priestley)

69. On a sunny day in 1909 car 54, having left the Guildhall via Cheap Street, turns into Stall Street. To the left of the tramcar is the Grand Pump Room Hotel. A little further down to the right are the famous Roman Baths. In the foreground, we see the Public Mineral Water Fountain, which was designed by Stephano Pieroni in 1859, but is in a somewhat overgrown state. There was originally a statue of King Bladud in the middle.
(P.C.Welland Coll.)

70. Further down Stall Street and still with car 54 on her journey to Oldfield Park, we see a delightful array of parked motor cars. All routes, except Newton and Weston, would use this as the outgoing stretch. After leaving Stall Street junction, they would then enter Southgate Street and proceed across the Old Bridge. In this photograph we can see Foster's Cash Tailors, Halfords and, in the foreground, F.W.Woolworth. This location is now occupied by HMV Video.
(Bath Reference Library)

TWERTON - GUILDHALL

71. Here is Car 6 on the Lower Bristol Road at Twerton terminus sometime in 1909. Motorman Fred Payne and his unknown conductor pose smartly for the cameraman. The high wall to the left of the car belonged to the GWR whose tracks it supports for trains to Bristol and London. Twerton in those days was a village but is now a suburb of Bath. (Mrs E.Derrick Coll.)

72. Car 55 stands on a sunny Sunday, 21st August 1938, at the Twerton terminus. Behind the car we view the Parochial School. One can imagine the conversation between the lady carrying the brolly and the gentleman with his hand on his hip. "Sorry George but after all these years I still cannot travel on that horseless carriage". "Oh Mildred". (M.J.O'Connor)

73. This is Sydenham Terrace, Lower Bristol Road and the year is 1903. This shows the permanent way workforce who were only paid four pence ha'penny (less than 2p) an hour! This must have been very hard work as there are no signs of mechanical help. A little way back to the left is Westmoreland Road, which will take the trams under the low railway bridge on their way to Oldfield Park. (G.Drew Coll.)

74. This is Oldfield Park junction taken on 9th February 1930 by Geoffrey Southerden who positioned himself in Westmoreland Road looking directly into Lower Bristol Road. The double decker from Twerton will continue to-wards the Old Bridge after which she will turn right into Dorchester Street. If we were to stand and look at this scene today we would be looking at Westward Motors Ltd. (G.N.Southerden)

75. Here we observe the lovely structure of the Old Bridge with cars 27 and 12 passing each other. Car 12 heads for Twerton whilst car 27, with an ample supply of passengers, heads towards Dorchester Street. To the left we can see the Cliff View Hotel and Restaurant. This scene was captured on 10th September 1937. (H.B.Priestley)

76. A seagull's view of the same bridge which shows the junction for Oldfield Park and Twerton to the left. The cars for Combe Down would continue underneath the cameraman on the Railway Bridge. Interestingly, car 53 is on the Twerton route and only on Sundays was this worked by single deckers. Car 51 approaches the city and will turn right into Dorchester Street which is behind the Full Moon Hotel. (Bath Reference Library)

77. Below the Abbey and the overhead is the Royal Literary and Scientific Institution and Museum, which was demolished in 1933 for road improvements (compare with picture 31). Car 2 is rounding the one-way system for tram-cars at Terrace Walk and will then continue into Orange Grove.
(Bristol Tramways & Carriage Co. Ltd.)

78. Having come round Orange Grove against the flow of traffic, car 15 approaches the terminus at Guildhall, although the stop was outside the Abbey. Note the feeder wire just behind the trolley arm. (W.S.Eades)

79. Earlier, the stop was outside the Guildhall itself, where car 22 has just departed for a return trip to Twerton, leaving car 18 and another at this busy central terminus in 1906. (P.C.Welland Coll.)

Cars should never be run so as to " cut " or interfere with a funeral procession, unless authorised to do so.

79 Sounding Gong—Motormen should sound the gong on approaching cars on the opposite track ; before crossings, intercepting streets, and on approaching vehicles on track ahead or on side of track.

Avoid sounding gong when approaching churches during hours of service, and when passing hospitals.

Do not unnecessarily sound gong at any time.

No gongs should be sounded when passing the Royal United Hospital in the Lower Boro' Walls, on the Weston and Newbridge Road routes, except in cases of necessity.

80 Head Lights—Motormen will be held responsible for the proper condition and illumination of head lights ; they should also see that the destination signs indicate correctly.

81 Power off the Line—In case the power is off the line the controller should be turned to the " off " position, the overhead switch opened and the light turned on. No attempt to start the car should be made until the lights burn brightly, and all cars going towards the Power Station should wait ½ minute after the lights are burning brightly, and all cars coming from the Power-house should wait one minute before an attempt is made to start the car.

It is very important that the controller should be turned entirely off while waiting for power, as it is impossible to turn the current on the line while the controllers of the cars are turned on.

82 Speed—Cars must never run ahead of the schedule time unless directed to do so by an authorised officer of the Company.

When passing Elementary Schools between 12 and 12-15 p.m., and between 4 and 4-45 p.m., Drivers must ring their bells frequently, to give children the necessary warning of an approaching car.

Drivers are required to enter and leave all points with caution, shutting off power, and running at a greatly reduced speed.

Drivers must run with caution on approaching bridges, curves, in going down grades, or while passing cars in slow motion, or car standing on the opposite track, or in passing vehicles standing near the track, schoolhouses, or any places where children are wont to congregate.

Extract from motorman's handbook

80. "One day you'll dress like me". Learner driver on car 33 waits politely for car 26 to cross the points. Motormen on driving instruction did so in their own time without being paid. The date is 2nd September 1933. (G.N.Southerden)

81. At the same location on 24th November 1935 car 53 works the Sunday duties to Twerton whilst another tram arrives from Combe Down about to pick up passengers for the Bathford route. (J.B.Appleby Coll.)

→

82. Car 53 again, this time working to Oldfield Park with the Twerton tram tucked in behind. The two tramcars offer rival advice as to the best alcoholic "pick-me-up"; note the fine ornamental lamp standard cum tramway traction pole. (W.A.Camwell)

83. From the Guildhall the route returned via Cheap Street and Stall Street, where car 24 is shown here destined for Twerton having just passed the pillars for the Abbey Churchyard. This spot today is now partially pedestrianised. (Bath Reference Library)

WESTON - G.W.R. STATION

84. A fine view shows car 14 in 1932 at the terminus ready for her run to the GWR Station with the motorman putting his mittens on. These saved the blackening of the hands from the brass hand brake and power handles. Note the magnetic track brake between the wheels. (P.G.Davey Coll.)

85. Just leaving the village is car 14 again, but much later, on 27th July 1938. She is just about to pass the grounds of the Royal United Hospital, formerly those of Manor House. On the left is R.Jones, Manor Road Dairy. Note the two extra upper deck lights. (H.B.Priestley)

86 Trolley Pole—Never run the trolley in the wrong direction except in cases of extreme necessity, and then very slowly and only for a short distance.

Never place the trolley wheel on the wire or take it off the wire when the controller is turned on.

87 Controllers—There are two controllers on each car. There are two handles for the controller, the 'reverse' handle, which regulates the direction in which the car runs, and the "controller" handle, which regulates the current feed into the motors.

When the reverse handle points forward the car will run forward. When it points backward the car will run backward.

The running notches are, No. 4 for slow speed, and No. 7 for fast speed. The other notches are, 1, 2, 3, 5 and 6 are starting notches, and the pointer should be held on them enough to give a gradual increase of speed (see Rule driving the car, paragraph 3).

The controller and reverse handles are interlocked, so that the controller handle cannot be moved unless the reverse is turned either forward or backward. The reverse handle cannot be moved unless the controller handle is set at "off." The reverse handle must be brought to the middle point in order to remove it.

Never leave the car without removing the controlling and reversing handles and opening the main switch.

88 Brakes—Both the double deck and single deck cars are equipped with the same kind of brakes, viz :—

    (1) The Westinghouse Newell Magnetic Track Brake.
    (2) The ordinary hand brake.

Before leaving the car-shed the Motorman should test the brakes, and any irregularity in their action should be reported immediately.

Except in an emergency the brakes should be applied gradually.

89 The Magnetic Brake—The Magnetic Brake should be used for coasting and for all stops in regular service on down gradients. The Magnetic Brake should not be used for entering or leaving points except in cases of emergency.

Extract from motorman's handbook

86. Car 10 creeps round from the Upper Bristol Road turning right into Nile Street. The track in the foreground swings left into Great Stanhope Street. Norfolk Crescent is behind the camera. (Bath Reference Library)

87. Cruising through Kingsmead Street is car 6, with the side destination board which would have read VIA ROYAL UNITED HOSPITAL. This stretch of track was controlled by lights because of single line working and were operated by the trolley arm hitting a frog. (S.Miles Davey)

88. The route arrives at Kingsmead Square where car 26 is possibly waiting for an oncoming tram to come through the single track section. Obviously a very early view as so many people are watching the camera. It is quite possible that the PW department has just cleared the tracks. (P.C.Welland Coll.)

89. A little further on than the previous view and car 3 crosses the Square during 1935 before turning into Westgate Buildings. On the right is the present day Seven Dials complex. Fred Wright's tobacconist is now Scoff's Wholefood Bakery. The track area has now been paved over to make two separate thoroughfares. (S.G.Jackman)

91. Having arrived at the top of Southgate Street we pull in behind car 9 which is passing car 25 on her way back to Weston. The fashionable ladies of 1925 are hesitant to cross the tracks which become single here. On the right can be seen the splendid entrance to St. James' Church which was destroyed by enemy action in World War II. (Bath Reference Library)

90. In 1925 we see Car 15 turning into Westgate Buildings. At the top of the staircase was the Company's permanent advert which read TRAVEL BY BATH TRAMWAYS GREEN TORPEDOES. This gives a good view of the top deck seating layout and shows that the seats situated on the canopy above the motorman were designed for three passengers. The shop on the corner, A.H.Barnes, is now the Bottoms Up Wine Store and that on the right is the Pizza Hut. (Bath Reference Library)

92. Co-author, Peter Davey, was told: "Stand still and don't move!", having just got off the train from Bristol. Double and single tramcars together with a new Bristol bus were all lined up for an instant in Dorchester Street during the last week of operation. The Newton route was the first to be replaced by buses on 29th October 1938. Car 24 will terminate outside the GWR Station. (S.Miles Davey)

93. At the terminus car 2 waits in front of the footbridge which connected the Royal Hotel with the railway station. Patrons from the hotel used this as a quick route to and from the trains. It seems that this was its sole use. Some excellent enamel adverts for BOVRIL and DEWAR'S WHISKY are seen behind the tram. (P.G.Davey Coll.)

94. At the same location car 4 waits for her next duty, but the footbridge to the Royal Hotel has now gone. Note the GWR coaches parked on the embankment at the east end of the station on a rather wet afternoon. (P.G.Davey Coll.)

ROLLING STOCK

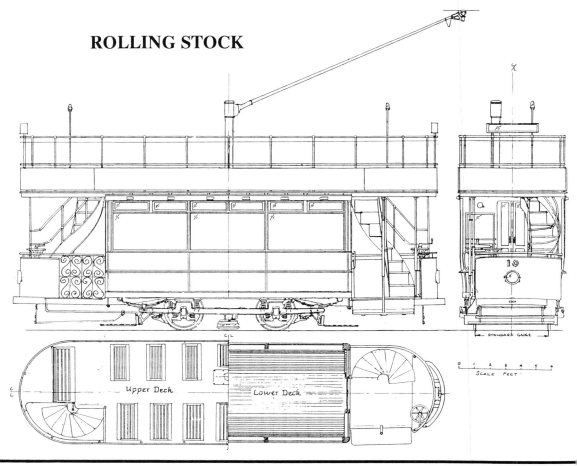

Cars 1 - 26 were built in 1903; cars 27 - 34 followed in 1904. Bodies were built by G.F.Milnes, Birkenhead, with seating for 22 lower deck and 33 upper deck. Trucks were of girder type by Busch of Bautzen, Saxony, to Milnes' specification. The motors and controllers were by British Westinghouse. Cars 50 - 53 were built in 1903 and cars 54 - 55 were constructed in 1904. Bodies were by G.F.Milnes, Birkenhead, with seating for 30. Trucks, motors and controllers were identical to the equipment supplied for the double deck vehicles.

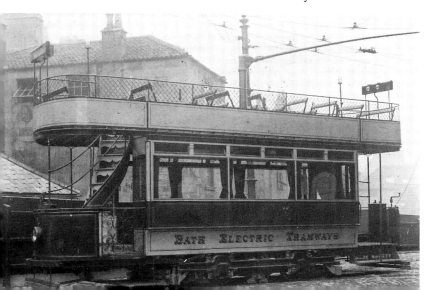

95. Typical standard double decker, car 9 is depicted in as delivered condition.
(C.G.Maggs Coll.)

96. This 1938 view illustrates car 25 in her final
state. It is a tribute to the staff of Bath Electric
Tramways that these vehicles were maintained
so well and kept in such splendid condition.
(W.A.Camwell)

97. Typical single decker of first series, car 52
is shown in original condition.
(P.C.Welland Coll.)

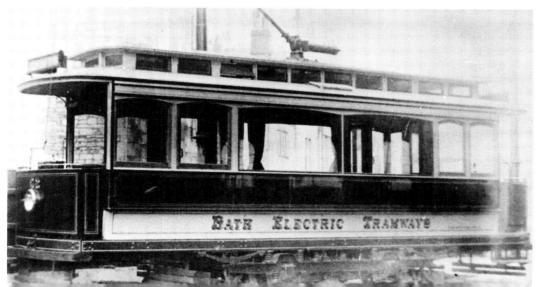

98. Cars 50 - 53 were delivered with angular dashes as demonstrated by car 52 seen on the Lower Bristol Road. (S.Miles Davey)

99. Cars 54 - 55 were delivered with rounded dashes. Car 55 is captured on film outside the Abbey on 26th July 1936. (H.B.Priestley)

100. An excellent broadside view of car 54 shows the compact nature of these trams. The 6 ft./1828mm wheelbase Milnes girder truck was rare in this country. They were manufactured at Bautzen in Germany by the Busch Maschinenfabrik AG. As well as Bath, these trucks were supplied for the standard gauge South Lancashire system and for the narrow gauge lines at Camborne in Cornwall and Kirkcaldy in Scotland. (C.Carter)

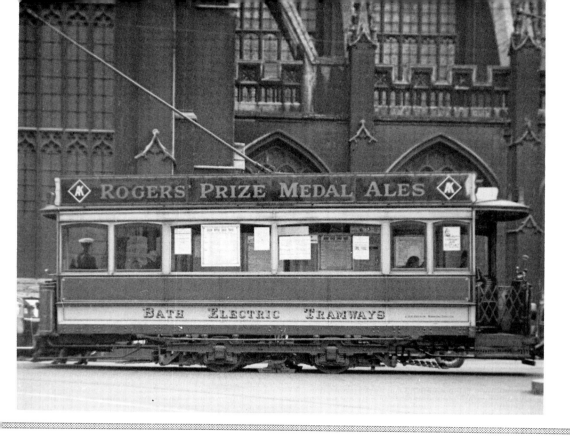

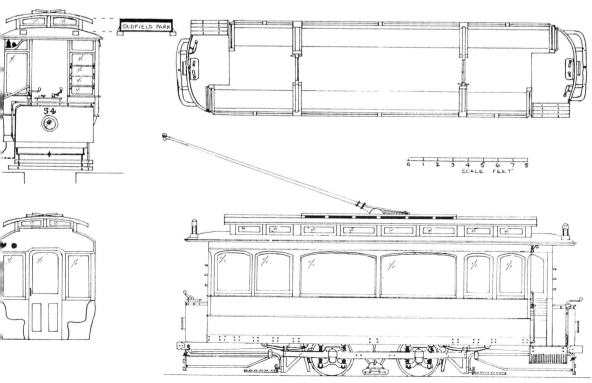

OLDFIELD PARK

54

0 1 2 3 4 5 6 7 8
SCALE FEET

101. Sadly, no photograph of the water car has come to light except for part of her showing up behind Car 9. Part of the lettering on the side is visible. She was reported to have looked like a "Torpedo Boat Destroyer", thought to have been possibly longer than the standard tram and painted overall in black. The staff called her the *Black Maria* and she was probably built locally by the company itself on a truck identical to the others. It was used as a sweeper car and a snow clearer, and may also have been used as a railgrinder.
(H.B.Priestley)

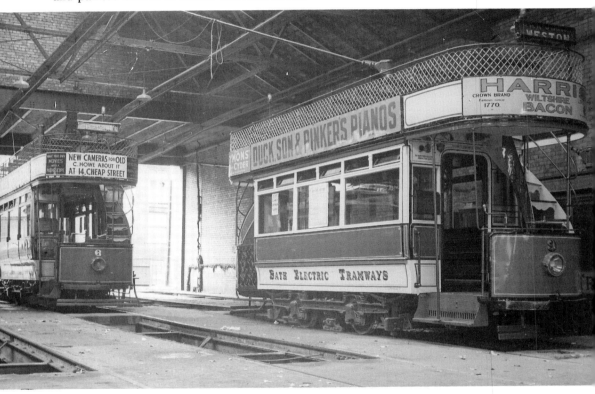

102. Car 10 was the fleet's maintenance car and she is seen here on such duties near to the terminus on Combe Down, with the curtains drawn. She was also used, amazingly, on the Oldfield Park route. For this operation the trolley pole was disconnected and one from a single deck was used instead. The top deck lights and destination boxes were taken off, so that she could travel under the GWR low bridge in Westmoreland Road. For grinding work water was taken from four barrels, which were stored in the lower saloon to keep the carborundum blocks cool, and one of these can be seen between the wheels. Note the BET monogram on the waistpanel.
(C.G.Maggs Coll.)

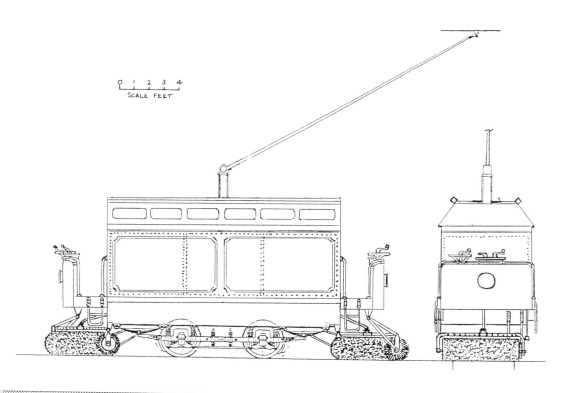

SCALE FEET
0 1 2 3 4

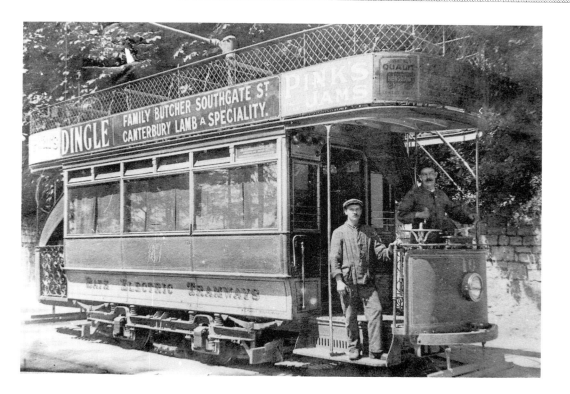

103. On 19th July 1909 car 32 is captured in front of the Abbey decorated for the Bath Pageant and was used as an enquiry bureau. It appears, for easy entry, that the centre handrail has been removed. At various intervals she would tour the city and then return to this disused loop outside the Guildhall. (P.G.Davey Coll.)

104. Car 6 stands outside Walcot Street Depot in 1923 having been decorated for the Bath Rotary Club to collect coppers for the Mayor's Distress Fund. A charabanc was also decorated and this toured the areas of the city not covered by the trams. It is thought that the money went to the unemployed ex servicemen's organisation and the total counted was two hundred and thirty pounds, six shillings and ninepence (£230.34) over a ten day period. (C.G.Maggs Coll.)

ACCIDENTS

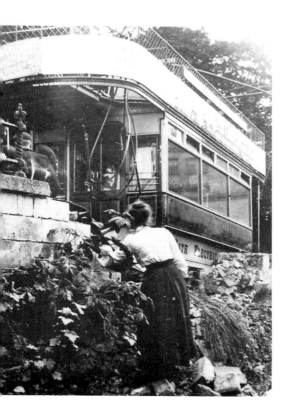

105. Oops! The crew were asked to drop in for tea - and they took the invitation literally! This was soon after the opening in 1904. Somehow the unfortunate vehicle has become derailed coming down Wellsway. Above the main advertisement is a destination board which reads COMBE DOWN VILLAGE. Note the staircase and dash have all been destroyed.
(C.G.Maggs Coll.)

106. Outside Bayer's Corset Factory, Lower Bristol Road, car 15, returning from Twerton, was attacked by a Pickford's truck on the wrong side of the road and came off the worse as its canopy has been torn off. One of the crew can be seen beside the tram.
(C.G.Maggs Coll.)

107. On 3rd July 1933 two trams were in collision at the bottom of Wells Road. Car 6, on the left, was driven by motorman W.D.Hobbs. He had reached as far as Hayesfield Park and then slipped on wet tar, due to the heat wave. Even though the driver released sand, the tram's wheels lost adhesion, so she ran back down Wells Road. The driver of car 18, motorman Harper, suddenly saw an unavoidable situation and sensibly stopped, and reversed slowly to lessen the impact, having made sure he had run through the tram to the other end! Two passengers on the runaway car were killed, and both cars travelled 150 yards/137 metres after the crash. (A.Gallop Coll.)

Bath Electric Tramways, Ltd.

....

Superintendent's Office,
Walcot Street,

BATH *9 March* 190 4

Sir,—

    I have to notify you that

a van

belonging to you and driven by Mr F. Culverhouse

came in collision with this Company's Car No. 18

at Lower Bond Walls *on*

8th *inst at* 7-25 pm.

....

   As I hold you responsible for the damage,
I give this notice that any inquiry you think
proper may be made.

     Yours obediently,
      R. D. McCARTER,
        Engineer and Manager.

Mr Bowler
13 Combe St
Bath

UNIFORMS

108. Showing their smart turnout are Motorman H.Brewer and Conductor T.Tavener standing in front of car 15 at Weston terminus. Note the points bar lodged in front of the staircase and also note hanging from the canopy, the route number board showing 3. All conductors' equipment included a bell punch, whistle, nippers for transfer tickets and a cash bag. Mr Brewer is wearing gaiters and has a pocket watch attached by a chain.
(C.G.Maggs Coll.)

Various badges from the collection of coauthor, Paul Welland, show the styles used at the end of the system. The top scroll was used for the headwear and greatcoat lapels. The buttons were the same for all their clothing but those for inspectors were brass, but to the same design. Also shown are two chrome badges showing their status. (B.K.Lewis)

END OF THE LINE

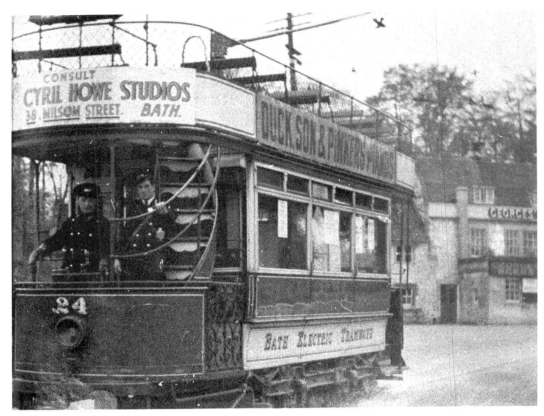

109. On 29th October 1938 car 24 has arrived at Newton terminus on the last outgoing journey. So as to avoid vandalism and souvenir hunters, she returned to the city empty after all her passengers were transferred to a waiting motor bus, much to their amazement and annoyance. (C.G.Maggs Coll.)

110. The evening of 6th May 1939 and car 1 runs through Lambridge with the last night revellers on top. Motorman Bill Gingell, brother of Wilf Gingell, wonders whether he will actually reach the Guildhall whilst driving the last passenger car from Bathford.
(Bath Chronicle)

SCRAPPING

111. Opposite St.Martin's Hospital in Midford Road two special sidings were laid into an area designated to cremate the majority of the fleet. Car 2 is at the far end of the longer of the two whilst car 53 waits on the other track. (W.Vaughan-Jenkins)

112. A school boy's dream comes true - Gerald Bath takes control not long before car 55 is scrapped. Evelyn Bath has accompanied her son. (G.Bath Coll.)

113. Lined up awaiting their fate are cars 53 and 19 with many other unidentified trams. (S.Miles Davey)

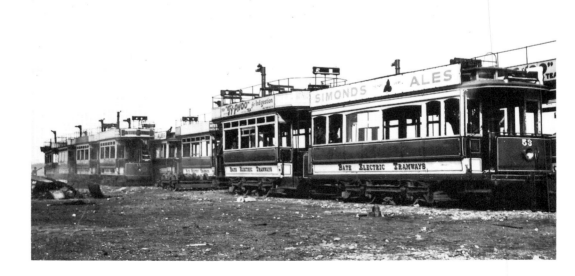

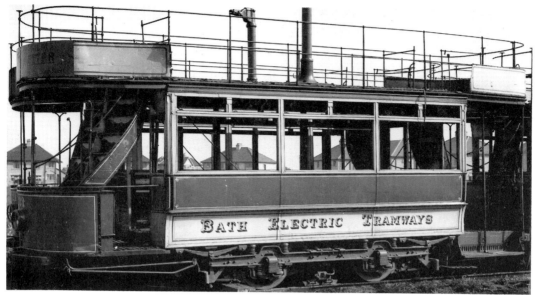

114. Cars 33 and 21 - the latter had experimental destination rollers fitted in the 1920s on to the centre windows on both sides. This photograph shows a further stage in the tramcar breaking. (S.Miles Davey)

115. Viewed from the top of a double decker, we can see car 53's unusual roof layout beside a stripped top deck. (S.Miles Davey)

116. Periscopes up! Car 16's trolley mast has been discarded and all the trams are nearing their final destination. Some of the trolley arms were recycled as radio (or "wireless" in those days) aerials. (W. Vaughan-Jenkins)

117. Maybe the last of the city's tramcars, stripped of all her pride, is now engulfed and disappears into the haze of time. Her memories held by the skies of Bath. A notice on the tram would have said NO SMOKING ALLOWED INSIDE THE CAR! (C.G. Maggs Collection)

FINALE

118. More buses than trams, as one of the last of the single deckers is almost obscured by the invasion of Bath's new mode of transportation at the Walcot Street tram depot. Buses will soon take over the whole system and then all the environmentally friendly trams will disappear. (P.G.Davey Coll.)

119. Here we see both authors' combined items of memorabilia - the power controller handle which once belonged to car 22 (the official last tram on 6th May 1939), the top destination box which adorned car 32 and the bottom box which belonged to car 4. (P.G.Davey)

120. This rosette, still in situ on the wall in Southgate Street appears to be the last of its kind in the city. Sadly, no Bath tramcar exists and after 6th May 1939 the city's transport was taken over by the Bristol Tramways and Carriage Company Ltd. The only other known connection with the tram era is the channelling for the overhead wires, which may still be found in the roof of the Walcot Street depot. As we walked out we heard a hiss - and both looked up. (P.G.Davey)

MP Middleton Press

Easebourne Lane, Midhurst. West Sussex. GU29 9AZ   Tel: 01730 813169   Fax: 01730 812601

..... Write or telephone for our latest list .....

BRANCH LINES
Branch Line to Allhallows
Branch Lines to Alton
Branch Lines around Ascot
Branch Lines around Bodmin
Branch Line to Bude
Branch Lines around Canterbury
Branch Lines to East Grinstead
Branch Lines around Effingham Jn
Branch Line to Fairford
Branch Line to Hawkhurst
Branch Lines to Longmoor
Branch Line to Lyme Regis
Branch Line to Lynton
Branch Lines around Midhurst
Branch Line to Minehead
Branch Lines to Newport
Branch Line to Padstow
Branch Lines around Portmadoc 1923-46
Branch Lines around Porthmadog 1954-94
Branch Lines to Seaton & Sidmouth
Branch Line to Selsey
Branch Lines around Sheerness
Branch Line to Southwold
Branch Line to Swanage
Branch Lines to Torrington
Branch Lines to Tunbridge Wells
Branch Line to Upwell
Branch Lines around Weymouth

LONDON SUBURBAN RAILWAYS
Caterham and Tattenham Corner
Clapham Jn. to Beckenham Jn.
Crystal Palace and Catford Loop
East London Line
Holborn Viaduct to Lewisham
Lines aound Wimbledon
London Bridge to Addiscombe
Mitcham Junction Lines
South London Line
West Croydon to Epsom
West London Line
Willesden Junction to Richmond
Wimbledon to Epsom

STEAMING THROUGH
Steaming through Cornwall
Steaming through East Sussex
Steaming through the Isle of Wight
Steaming through Surrey
Steaming through West Hants
Steaming through West Sussex

GREAT RAILWAY ERAS
Ashford from Steam to Eurostar
Festiniog in the Fifties

COUNTRY BOOK
Brickmaking in Sussex

SOUTH COAST RAILWAYS
Ashford to Dover
Bournemouth to Weymouth
Brighton to Eastbourne
Brighton to Worthing
Chichester to Portsmouth
Dover to Ramsgate
Ryde to Ventnor
Worthing to Chichester

SOUTHERN MAIN LINES
Bromley South to Rochester
Charing Cross to Orpington
Crawley to Littlehampton
Dartford to Sittingbourne
East Croydon to Three Bridges
Epsom to Horsham
Exeter to Barnstaple
Exeter to Tavistock
Faversham to Dover
Haywards Heath to Seaford
London Bridge to East Croydon
Orpington to Tonbridge
Sittingbourne to Ramsgate
Swanley to Ashford
Tavistock to Plymouth
Tonbridge to Hastings
Victoria to Bromley South
Waterloo to Windsor
Woking to Portsmouth
Woking to Southampton
Yeovil to Exeter

COUNTRY RAILWAY ROUTES
Bath to Evercreech Junction
Bournemouth to Evercreech Jn
Burnham to Evercreech Junction
Croydon to East Grinstead
East Kent Light Railway
Fareham to Salisbury
Frome to Bristol
Guildford to Redhill
Porthmadog to Blaenau
Reading to Basingstoke
Reading to Guildford
Redhill to Ashford
Salisbury to Westbury
Strood to Paddock Wood
Taunton to Barnstaple
Westbury to Bath
Woking to Alton

TROLLEYBUS CLASSICS
Croydon's Trolleybuses
Hastings Trolleybuses
Woolwich & Dartford Trolleybuses

TRAMWAY CLASSICS
Aldgate & Stepney Tramways
Bath Tramways
Bournemouth & Poole Tramways
Brighton's Tramways
Bristol's Tramways
Camberwell & W. Norwood Tramways
Croydon's Tramways
Dover's Tramways
East Ham & West Ham Tramways
Eltham & Woolwich Tramways
Embankment & Waterloo Tramways
Exeter & Taunton Tramways
Greenwich & Dartford Tramways
Hampstead & Highgate Tramways
Hastings Tramways
Holborn & Finsbury Tramways
Ilford & Barking Tramways
Kingston & Wimbledon Tramways
Lewisham & Catford Tramways
Maidstone & Chatham Tramways
North Kent Tramways
Portsmouth's Tramways
Reading's Tramways
Seaton & Eastbourne Tramways
Southampton Tramways
Southend-on-sea Tramways
Stamford Hill Tramways
Thanet's Tramways
Victoria & Lambeth Tramways
Walthamstow & Leyton Tramways
Wandsworth & Battersea Tramways

OTHER RAILWAY BOOKS
Garraway Father & Son
Industrial Railways of the South East
London Chatham & Dover Railway
War on the Line

MILITARY BOOKS
Battle over Portsmouth
Battle over Sussex 1940
Blitz Over Sussex 1941-42
Bognor at War
Bombers over Sussex 1943-45
Military Defence of West Sussex
Secret Sussex Resistance

WATERWAY ALBUMS
Hampshire Waterways
Kent and East Sussex Waterways
London's Lost Route to the Sea
London to Portsmouth Waterway
Surrey Waterways

BUS BOOK
Eastbourne Bus Story

SOUTHERN RAILWAY
● VIDEO ●
War on the Line

96